Thomas Edison

Great American Inventor

by Shelley Bedik

SCHOLASTIC INC.

New York Toronto London Auckland Sydney

For Simon, my best invention yet!

Photo Credits

Front cover: photo: U.S. Department of the Interior, National Park Service, Edison National Historic Site; detail from vote recorder diagram: Culver Pictures.

Back cover: Consolidated Edison Company of New York.

Brown Brothers: p. 27; Consolidated Edison Company of New York: p. 23; Culver Pictures: pp. 1, 3, 6, 8, 32, and detail of vote recorder diagram, pp. 3–32; from the Collection of Henry Ford Museum & Greenfield Village: pp. 5, 13, 17, 20; National Museum of History and Technology, Smithsonian Institution: p. 24; U.S. Department of the Interior, National Park Service, Edison National Historic Site: pp. 9, 10, 14, 19, 26, 28, 31.

ISBN 0-590-48357-9

12 11 10 9 8 7 6 5 4 3 2 1   5 6 7 8 9/9 0/0

Printed in the U.S.A.   24

First Scholastic printing, February 1995

Thomas Edison's birthplace in Milan, Ohio.

THOMAS ALVA EDISON was born on February 11, 1847. At that time, people rode in carriages, not cars. They used candles or gas lamps, not electric lights. They sent messages through letters, not telephones. Cars, electric lights, and telephones had not been invented yet. Most people did not know much about electricity at all.

Thomas Alva Edison was said to be a very curious young boy. He wanted to find out all he could about the world around him. He loved to ask questions such as, "Is there a way to make people fly?" and, "Why does a goose sit on her eggs?"

There are many stories about Thomas Edison's childhood. Some people say he tried experiments to find the answers to his questions. They say he made a friend swallow worms to make her fly like a bird, and that he sat on a nest of goose eggs to hatch them. No one knows if these stories really happened. If they did, Edison's first experiments did not work very well!

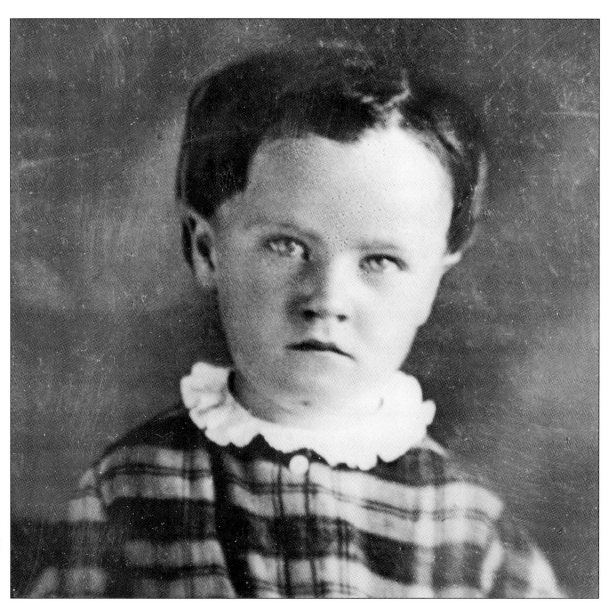

Some people called Thomas Edison "Al" after his middle name, "Alva."

The boyhood home of Thomas Edison in Port Huron, Michigan.

When Thomas was seven years old, his family moved to Port Huron, Michigan. He started school for the first time. Thomas was often sick with ear infections. He may have had a hard time hearing his teacher. It has been said that Thomas's teacher talked with his parents about Thomas not paying attention in class.

Nancy Edison, Thomas Edison's mother.

The Edisons tried sending Thomas
to different schools, but he still had problems
learning. Mrs. Edison had been a schoolteacher.
She knew that her son was smart. So she took
Thomas out of school and from that time on,
gave him his lessons at home.

Young Thomas with his sister Tannie.

Thomas Edison loved to read. When he was nine, his mother gave him a science book with experiments in it. Thomas set up his own laboratory with chemicals, wires, and other things he needed. He tried every experiment in the book.

Thomas once sold 1,000 newspapers in one day!

Thomas Edison got a job when he was just twelve years old. He sold newspapers, books, and candy to passengers onboard a train. A conductor let him set up a laboratory in the baggage car. Thomas worked on experiments in his free time.

One day, Thomas tried to climb onto the train with his hands full of newspapers. The conductor grabbed him by the ears to stop him from falling. Thomas said he felt something "snap" inside his head. He made it safely onto the train. But as he grew older, it was harder and harder for him to hear.

This train is similar to the one Edison worked on as a boy.

The Mount Clemens, Michigan, train station where Thomas saved a young boy's life.

Then Thomas did something very important. He saved a child's life! A little boy was playing on the train tracks. Thomas pulled him out of the way of a moving freight train. The boy's father was very grateful. He promised to teach Thomas how to be a telegraph operator.

The telegraph was a new way of using electricity to send messages in code from place to place. Later, Edison traveled to many cities working as a telegraph operator.

Thomas Edison as a young man.

Everywhere he went, Edison looked closely at machines that used electricity. He read books and studied drawings. He still wanted to understand the way everything worked! Edison started filling notebooks with drawings and ideas of his own.

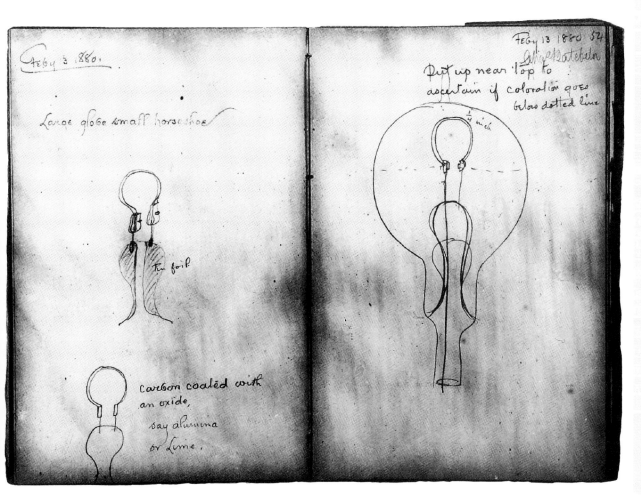

Feby 3 1880.

Large globe small horseshoe

Tin foil

Carbon coaled with
an oxide,
say alumina
or Lime.

Feby 13 1880 54
Chas Batchelor

Put up near Top to
ascertain if coloration goes
below dotted line

¼ inch

Sketches for the lightbulb from Thomas Edison's notebooks.

Thomas Edison's electric vote recorder.

In 1868, Edison invented a machine to count votes. But when he showed the electric vote recorder to the people in the government, they didn't want to use it. Edison was disappointed. He made himself a promise — "I would never again waste any time in inventing anything that is not of general usefulness to the people, or that people do not want and will not buy."

For the next few years, Edison worked hard to improve the telegraph machine. He also found time to invent the electric pen. He was twenty-nine years old when he built a laboratory in Menlo Park, New Jersey. Some people called it Edison's "invention factory." He hired people who had important skills and knowledge to work with him.

Edison and his staff inside the Menlo Park Laboratory.

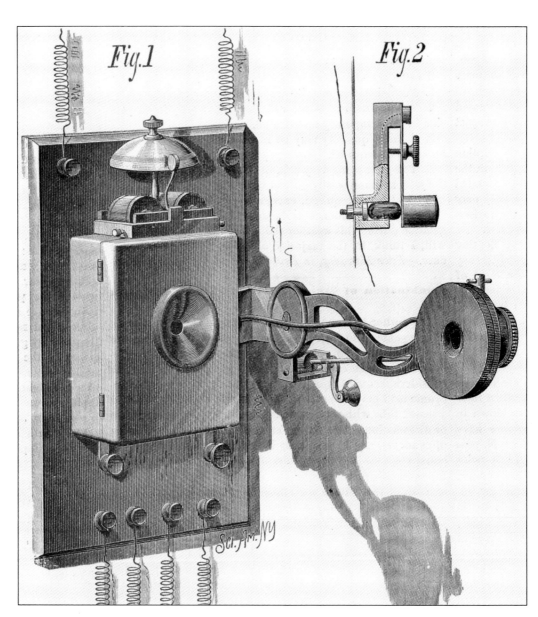

Edison's new and improved telephone.

Sometimes Edison worked to improve other people's inventions. Alexander Graham Bell invented the telephone. Edison added a better microphone. Soon many people were using the telephone that these two inventors created.

Edison showed his tinfoil phonograph at the White House.

Edison also came up with ideas for inventions that were new and different. His favorite idea came when he was trying to find a way to record telegraph messages. He created a machine that could record sounds, called a phonograph.

From the Laboratory

of

Thomas A. Edison,

Orange NJ. Aug 14 1918.

Dear Carty

In reply to your question, let me say that I was the first person to speak into the first phonograph. The first words spoken by me into the original model, and that were reproduced were "Mary had a little lamb" and the other three lines of that verse.

Yours sincerely

Thos A Edison

Edison wrote this letter about the first words ever recorded.

Thomas Edison holding his "incandescent lamp."

Many scientists tried to invent a new kind of light. Thomas Edison finally did it. His lightbulb was his most famous invention. It used electricity instead of gas to bring light into people's homes. People began calling him "the Wizard of Menlo Park."

Edison built a huge new laboratory in West Orange, New Jersey. For many years, he worked on new ideas with teams of scientists and inventors. He experimented with batteries for cars. He tried to find ways to grow rubber plants in the United States. He even invented a machine to show movies.

Thomas Edison working on his motion picture projector.

Thomas Alva Edison died on October 18, 1931. Across the United States, lights were dimmed in honor of this great man.

Without Edison's inventions, our world would be a very different place. So the next time you turn on a light, listen to music, or go to a movie theater, remember Thomas Edison, one of America's greatest inventors.